Hummingbird and Heron

retold by Jay Parker
illustrated by Jiri Tibor Novak

Harcourt
SCHOOL PUBLISHERS

Printed in Mexico

ISBN 10: 0-15-350641-5
ISBN 13: 978-0-15-350641-3

Ordering Options
ISBN 10: 0-15-350599-0 (Grade 2 On-Level Collection)
ISBN 13: 978-0-15-350599-7 (Grade 2 On-Level Collection)
ISBN 10: 0-15-357822-X (package of 5)
ISBN 13: 978-0-15-357822-9 (package of 5)

2 3 4 5 6 7 8 9 10   050   15 14 13 12 11 10 09 08 07

Long ago, both Heron and Hummingbird ate fish. Hummingbird, who was tiny and fast, ate tiny fish. Heron, who was big and slow, ate big fish.

One day, Hummingbird shared with Heron what he had been thinking.

"There may not always be enough fish for all the birds like us," said Hummingbird.

"There may not be," agreed Heron.

"Perhaps only one of us should eat fish," Heron suggested.

"Shall we have a race to decide who that will be?" asked Hummingbird.

"That seems fair," said Heron.

The birds decided they would race to a tree they both knew.

"It's a long way from here, though," said big, slow Heron. "It is clear to me that the race will take four days."

"I accept that," Hummingbird said, thinking he could get there much faster.

They started the race the next
morning. Heron flew straight ahead.
Hummingbird flew in circles around
his friend.

Then Hummingbird flew down to some flowers.

"What are you doing?" Heron called from above.

"I am drinking sweet nectar," called Hummingbird.

"What's that?" asked Heron.

"The honey inside the flowers," Hummingbird called back.

Heron didn't hear Hummingbird's answer. He had already flown on ahead of Hummingbird.

Suddenly, Hummingbird realized Heron was not in sight. Off he raced to join his friend again. That was how the race continued.

Heron flew on and on, straight ahead. Hummingbird stopped every time he saw flowers. Then he raced to pass Heron again.

Hummingbird stopped to rest at night, too. He slept near flowers and drank sweet nectar for breakfast. Then he raced to catch up with Heron, who just kept flying.

Hummingbird woke on the
last morning.

"It will take me only another half
hour to get to the tree," he thought.
"I wonder where Heron is."

When Hummingbird arrived, big, slow Heron was already at the tree. Heron won the race by flying without stopping while Hummingbird rested.

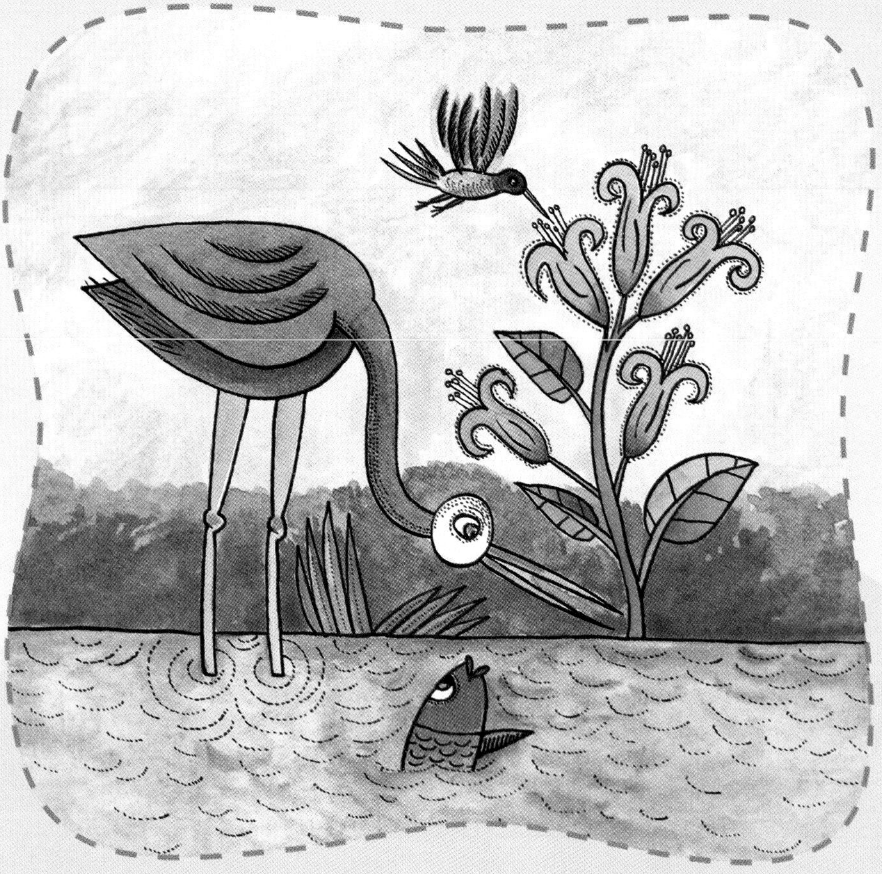

That is how Heron became the owner of all the fish in the rivers. It is also why Hummingbird flies among the flowers, drinking the sweet nectar he so enjoyed along the way.

Think Critically

1. Why did Hummingbird and Heron have a race?

2. What happened during Hummingbird and Heron's race?

3. Why do you think that Heron kept flying without stopping?

4. How do you think Hummingbird felt when he saw Heron at the tree?

5. At the beginning, which bird did you think would win the race? Why?

 Language Arts

Write a Story Write a story about two different animals that have a race.

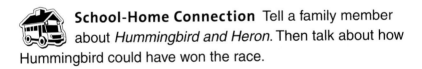 **School-Home Connection** Tell a family member about *Hummingbird and Heron.* Then talk about how Hummingbird could have won the race.